Includes 10 Fam...

Helping Children to Understand the Gospel

By Sally Michael, Jill Nelson, and Bud Burk

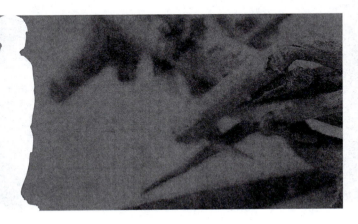

Pray for
Ed Kleiman
SMALL CLOUD MINISTRIES
www.praybold.org

Truth:78

Helping Children to Understand the Gospel
by Sally Michael, Jill Nelson, and Bud Burk

Copyright © 2009, 2011 by Next Generation Resources, Inc. and Jill Nelson. Illustrations Truth78. All rights reserved. No part of this publication may be reproduced in any form without written permission from Truth78.

Published in the United States by Truth78.

All Scripture quotations, unless otherwise noted, are from The Holy Bible, English Standard Version® (ESV®), copyright © 2001 by Crossway, a publishing ministry of Good News Publishers. Used by permission. All rights reserved.

ISBN: 978-0-9969870-3-5

Truth78.org · info@Truth78.org · 1-877-400-1414 · @Truth78org

Table of Contents

Part 1—Preparing Children for the Gospel....................................5
    Introduction..5
    The Sower..6
    The Seed...7
    The Soil...8
    How Do We Sow, Tend, and Harvest?............................9
    Stages of Growth..13
    Concluding Thoughts...22

Part 2—Presenting the Gospel to Children...................................24
    The Gospel Man Has Created..................................24
    The Gospel that Saves.......................................25
    Presenting the Gospel: In Context...........................26
    Presenting the Gospel: With Intentionality..................26
    Presenting the Gospel: At Every Opportunity with Prayer.....29

Part 3—Family Devotional: 10 Essential Truths of the Gospel................30
    Truth One: God is the sovereign Creator of all things.....31
    Truth Two: God created people for His glory...............35
    Truth Three: God is holy and righteous....................39
    Truth Four: Man is sinful.................................43
    Truth Five: God is just and is right to punish sin........48
    Truth Six: God is merciful. He is kind to undeserving sinners.............52
    Truth Seven: Jesus is God's holy and righteous Son........57
    Truth Eight: God put the punishment of sinners on Jesus...60
    Truth Nine: God offers the free gift of salvation to those who repent and believe in Jesus......................................66
    Truth Ten: Those who trust in Jesus will live to please Him and will receive the promise of eternal life—enjoying God forever in heaven........72

Summary of the Ten Gospel Truths..77
Recommended Titles for Further Reading....................................78
About Truth78...79

Part One: Preparing Children for the Gospel

Introduction

Two terra cotta planters sit side-by-side in a sunny corner of the yard. The same gardener has tended both pots, planting them at the same time with seeds from the same packet. Each pot has received the same careful attention—adequate water and sufficient sunlight. In one pot, the seeds have sprouted and the plants are growing to a full and healthy maturity. But the other pot still sits empty—the seeds have yielded nothing. Why the difference?

In one pot the seeds were planted in rocks, while in the other pot the seeds were planted in rich dark soil. In the end, the soil was the determining factor in this situation, because God has made seeds to grow in soil and not in rocks. And just as God has ordered certain conditions for growing seeds, He has also ordered certain conditions for growing His kingdom:

> A sower went out to sow. *4 And as he sowed, some seeds fell along the path, and the birds came and devoured them. 5 Other seeds fell on rocky ground, where they did not have much soil, and immediately they sprang up, since they had no depth of soil, 6 but when the sun rose they were scorched. And since they had no root, they withered away. 7 Other seeds fell among thorns, and the thorns grew up and choked them. 8 Other seeds fell on good soil and produced grain, some a hundredfold, some sixty, some thirty. 9 He who has ears, let him hear.* (Matthew 13:3b-9)

We know from the explanation of the parable Jesus gives later in the chapter that the seed is the Word of God and the soil is a person's heart. The Word of God is taught to all hearers, but it only takes true root in some hearts.

As we labor to sow the seeds of the Gospel to children in our classrooms and homes, this parable is very instructive for us. It presents us with the following questions to ponder:

- Who is the sower?
- What is the seed?
- What kind of soil is in the hearts of children?
- How do we sow, tend, and harvest?
- How do we lead a child to salvation, and what are the evidences of saving faith?

The Sower

> *No one can come to me unless the Father who sent me draws him.* (John 6:44a)

> *[18] All this is from God, who through Christ reconciled us to himself and gave us the ministry of reconciliation; [19] that is, in Christ God was reconciling the world to himself, not counting their trespasses against them, and entrusting to us the message of reconciliation. [20] Therefore, we are ambassadors for Christ, God making his appeal through us. We implore you on behalf of Christ, be reconciled to God.* (2 Corinthians 5:18-20)

Ultimately, the salvation of children is in God's sovereign hands. He chooses whom He wills and calls His own to Himself. Unless God is at work in a child's heart, all our efforts are in vain.

However, this does not mean that we are not to labor in this ministry. As believers we have the privilege of being God's instruments. We are laborers in God's vineyard, and God has "entrusted" us with this great privilege and awesome responsibility (1 Corinthians 3:4-9). We are to work in cooperation with God, who gives root to the seeds of Gospel truth we sow in the hearts of children.

As God's sowers, we are called to:

- Pray for the hearts of children, because without the Spirit of God working in them they cannot be saved (1 Corinthians 3:-5-7).
- Teach the Word of God diligently all the time, in all places, under all circumstances (Deuteronomy 6:7).

- Model a life of faith evidencing that we love the LORD our God with all our heart, all our soul, and all our might (Deuteronomy 6:5).

The Seed

So faith comes from hearing, and hearing through the word of Christ. (Romans 10:17)

The seed is the Gospel: the good news of Jesus. God has ordained that saving faith comes through the hearing of the Gospel through the proclamation of the Word (Romans 10:17). This "hearing" is a hearing that involves understanding the Word and embracing it as true. Without an understanding and embracing of the Gospel, there is no salvation.

In working with children, we sometimes fool ourselves into thinking that the method we use is what saves children; that it is in age-appropriate techniques we find success. While we do want to be age-appropriate in our teaching, this is not what saves. It is not the method but the message that saves (see Romans 1:16). And the message is this: Jesus Christ came to save sinners. Those who believe in Him are saved from the wrath of God and have eternal life (John 3:36). This Gospel saves children and adults alike.

When presenting the Gospel to children, it is important to emphasize that salvation is not based on anything they do, but on what Jesus accomplished on the cross. In the introduction to the *Firm Foundations* curriculum, Trevor McIlwain explains it this way:

> *The Gospel is not man accepting Jesus as his Savior, but that God accepted the Lord Jesus as the perfect and only Savior two thousand years ago. The Gospel is not man giving his heart to Jesus, but that Christ gave His life, His whole being, in the place of sinners. [. . .] The sinner is only to trust in what has already been done on his behalf.*[1]

---
1. McIlwain, Trevor and Nancy Everson. Firm Foundations: Creation to Christ. (Sanford, Fla.: New Tribes Mission, 1991), 12.

The Gospel proclamation begins with a proclamation of objective facts, but it also calls for a personal experience of trust in Jesus. There needs to be a personal embracing of Jesus as Savior; a receiving of Him as Redeemer and Lord and trusting in His finished work on the cross. This is saving faith.

The Soil

The soil into which this Gospel message is sown is the child's heart.

Like all men, children are born with a sin nature inherited from Adam. No one has to teach a baby to arch his back and cry when he is put into a car seat; he is acting out of his sin nature. And a toddler is expressing his inborn rebellious nature when he stamps his feet and says a defiant, "No!" Even so, there is often a tenderness and an openness in children to spiritual truth that is absent in many adults.

Most children are not yet "hardened" by the deceitfulness of sin (Hebrews 3:13), so they often respond to spiritual teaching eagerly. They love to hear the stories of the Bible and sing songs about Jesus—many young children are even eager to pray to receive Christ. Sometimes this is genuine saving faith, but often it is only a spiritual interest. We need to discern the difference between spiritual interest and saving faith. Spiritual interest may be a step on the journey toward salvation, but it is not salvation.

There are genuine conversions of young children, but many times we confuse spiritual interest with saving faith. It is easy to confuse childhood curiosity with conviction. Spiritual interest is a good thing and we should rejoice when we see it, but we need to acknowledge that it is not always saving faith.

When a child shows spiritual interest and a desire to pray to Jesus, we should encourage him to pray and "ask Jesus to work in your heart" or "ask Jesus to save you from your sins." These are good prayers, but they are not certain evidence of genuine faith in and of themselves. We should encourage young children to trust in Jesus and to receive Jesus and to pray prayers like these, but not give that child the assurance that he is "saved" when he has prayed a prayer like this. A particular prayer may or may not be an expression of genuine saving faith. We need to impress on children that the person who is truly trusting in Jesus will continue to trust in Jesus and to turn away from sin.

It is hard to discern what kind of heart soil the Word of God is falling on when it is sown on young hearts. Many children who profess to know Christ are not saved. A child may think he is saved, and his parents may think he is saved because a prayer was prayed. But if over time there is little interest in spiritual things—if he is bored in church; if he is attracted to the world—he may yet be unconverted. A period of time when there was spiritual interest is no guarantee that the soil was fertile. Persevering in faith is a sign of genuine faith. Wrongly presuming salvation upon a child's profession of faith can lead to spiritual neglect. Both the law and the Gospel should be kept continually in front of the child, no matter what profession he has made. A parent who has presumed salvation may not continue to pray for the child's salvation or continue to encourage the child to trust in Jesus, and instead treat the child as a Christian in need only of further sanctification. The dangers of fostering a false assurance in children should be clearly recognized.

The job of the sower is to keep the Gospel in front of the child—to keep sowing the Word of God upon every opportunity; to break up clumps of soil with discipline and training; and to water the seed with unceasing prayer.

How Do We Sow, Tend, and Harvest?

When we plant seeds, we read the instructions on the back of the seed packets. Correctly following the instructions helps the seeds to take root and flourish. Likewise, spiritual sowers do well to heed the counsel and wisdom God has given in His Word. Although He can work in spite of our error, God delights in wise sowing.

Sowing in Confidence

The first thing we notice about any seed packet is the picture on the front. For example, on a packet of green bean seeds there is typically a picture of a cluster of ripe plump beans. This gives us the hope of an outcome—high yields of fresh green beans.

God has also given us hope as well for our Gospel sowing in the hearts of children:

> *"So shall my word be that goes out from my mouth; it shall not return to me empty, but it shall accomplish that which I purpose, and shall succeed in the thing for which I sent it. (Isaiah 55:11)*

Because the Word of God is powerful, there is a reasonable assurance that when He calls us to sow the Gospel, there will be a harvest of some sort. Not every child will be saved, but there is hope of a good yield from our labors (see 2 Corinthians 9:6).

Proper Conditions That Make for Growth

If we throw seeds in the ground but ignore the growing conditions, we will either end up with no plant or with a very unhealthy plant. Rather, we must strive to cultivate the proper growing conditions so that the seed is more likely to take root.

We must also be intentional in cultivating the soil when sowing spiritual seed. If we want the Gospel message to be understood and embraced, we should create an environment where the Gospel will flourish. A child without rules or discipline will have trouble embracing the Gospel. He has not learned that rules are non-negotiable, that there are consequences to actions, or that authority must be respected. Why would he ever believe God is sovereign over all His creation? Or the Ten Commandments are God's absolute rules of conduct? Or even that wrongdoing results in punishment—that he needs a Savior because hell is real?

We are so afraid of being labeled "legalistic" or "fundamentalistic" that we don't give children behavioral expectations or even moral standards. In a society that is afraid to upset the fragile egos of children, the concept of total depravity is lost. In abandoning the truth of our sinful and helpless condition, we have hardened the soil of children's hearts so that the Gospel becomes meaningless to them. Because they are "okay," they don't need a Savior.

Children need rules. They need to see that their sinful hearts rebel against standards and that they are unable to fulfill the expectations of proper conduct. They need to know the law of God so that they can understand the grace of the Gospel. John Calvin explained the law as preparation for the Gospel. Its function is to call the conscience into judgment and alarm it with fear.[2] Children will never love the atoning work of Christ on the cross if they don't understand how much they need a Savior.

We have to be willing to do what needs to be done in this physical world so that the rescue of the Gospel can be seen as glorious. To that end, we have to train diligently, providing experiences to reinforce spiritual truth. We have to lead and be in charge—to be courageous and do the hard things, allowing our children to experience some discomfort and even turmoil in this world in the hope that they will experience joy in the next. It is better for a child to learn a heart lesson, though it cause him temporary pain, than for him to ignorantly follow a path leading to eternal pain.

Double digging is a gardening technique that helps produce healthy plants. In this, the gardener removes the top 12 inches of the soil with a spade and then loosens the harder, hidden subsoil with a fork, breaking up the compacted clumps of soil until it is softened for growing roots.

Sometimes a child's heart may have deeply compacted soil as well. Sometimes the surface is very soft, loose, pliable, but the subsoil below the surface is hard—rebellious, self-centered, and encrusted with love for the world. It takes some hard cultivating to break open these deep-seated clumps of resistance and apathy. Consider the careful work of Reverend Richard Cecil, an English clergyman of the 1800s, as he endeavored to help his daughter understand the meaning of faith:

---

2. Metzger, Will. *Tell the Truth*. (Downers Grove, Ill.: InterVarsity Press, 2002), 62.

My little daughter was playing one day with a few beads, which seemed to delight her wonderfully. Her whole soul seemed to be absorbed in her beads. I said, "My dear, you have some pretty beads there." "Yes, papa." "And you seem to be vastly pleased with them." "Yes, papa."

"Well now, throw them into the fire." The tears started into her eyes. She looked earnestly at me, as though she ought to have a reason for such a cruel sacrifice. "Well, my dear, do as you please, but you know I never told you to do anything which I did not think would be good for you."

She looked at me a few moments longer, and then summoning up all her fortitude, her breast heaving with the effort, she dashed them into the fire. "Well," said I, "there let them lie; you shall hear more about them at another time, but say no more about them now."

Some days after, I bought her a box full of larger beads, and toys of the same kind. When I returned home, I opened the treasure, and set it before her; she burst into tears with joy. "Those, my child," said I, "are yours, because you believed me, when I told you it would be better for you to throw those two or three paltry beads into the fire. Now, that has brought you this treasure.

"But now, my dear, remember, as long as you live, what faith is. I did all this to teach you the meaning of FAITH. You threw your beads away when I bade you, because you had faith in me that I never advised you but for your good. Put the same trust in God. Believe everything that he says in his word. Whether you understand it or not, have faith in him that he means your good."[3]

The deep lessons hurt, but they are necessary for the Gospel to take a strong root in a child's heart. We live in a culture that

---

3. Walker, Charles. Repentance and Faith. (Birmingham, Ala.: Solid Ground Christian Books, 2006), 18-19.

esteems comfort, but in this we have our values reversed. It is much better for a child to learn a heart lesson though it cause him temporary pain, so that he might one day know the eternal joys of Christ in heaven.

Understanding the Growth Process

A green bean seed packet typically states that it will take 7-10 days for the seeds to germinate and 58 days until beans are ready to be harvested from mature plants. Fifty-eight days seems like a long time to wait to eat fresh green beans, but this growth is a process that cannot be rushed. God has His timing for all things.

Children are like plants—they grow in God-ordained stages, and it is wise to be attentive to those stages. They are not yet adults and do not yet have adult reasoning capabilities or maturity (1 Corinthians 13:11). A wise sower knows the stages of growth and nurtures the plant according to each stage's unique needs.

Stages of Growth

At each stage of plant growth, the gardener uses different techniques to meet the unique needs of the plant. A sprout and a mature plant receive very different treatment. Children also must be tended differently according to the conditions of their hearts and their spiritual interest and maturity. We must learn to recognize the stages of growth so we can tend hearts faithfully. The following stages outlined here are described (age, key terms, and our role) by Art Murphy in *The Faith of a Child*.

The Discovering Stage[4]

Age: birth to five years

Key Terms: first impressions, positive feelings, foundation building, sensory motor experiences.

---

4. Murphy, Art. *The Faith of a Child*. (Chicago: Moody Press, 2000), 60-62.

Our Role: cultivator—preparing the soil for seeds that will be planted later

This stage is best described as "the process of storing new information." During this first stage of life, a child stores huge amounts of information every day.[5]

This is the "information gathering stage." The children are like sponges soaking up everything around them through their *senses* and through their *emotions*. They are absorbing information rapidly.

This is the stage at which to build in children an arsenal of Bible stories and memory verses, a foundation of Biblical knowledge and a foundation of trust. Also, modeling must be intentional as the emotions children feel at this time about God, the Bible, and the church will shape their impressions of spiritual things later in life. The feelings a child experiences when he is with you will influence his impression of God. Children at this age will believe what you tell them just because you tell them; this is why it is so easy to get them to pray "the sinner's prayer."

The Discerning Stage[6]

Age: four to eight years

Key Terms: gathering facts, exploring the Bible, curiosity, asking questions

Our Role: planter—planting seeds through teaching, modeling, observing, answering

Unlike a preschooler, a child in the early elementary years begins to question things. He is beginning to do some thinking for himself instead of just absorbing what he is told. The constant "why" and "how" questions will, at times, be very difficult or even impossible to answer. But the questions should be welcomed.

At this stage we should give children the biblical answers for the questions we can answer and admit that we don't know the

---
5. Murphy, Art. *The Faith of a Child.* (Chicago: Moody Press, 2000), 60.
6. Ibid, 62-63.

answers to some of their questions. Cultivate the dialogue. The constant discussion with 4-8 year olds is an important opportunity to correct misconceptions and to help children really grasp the importance of the Gospel. It is very important to make sure that by early elementary years a child understands the Gospel—not just that he has a knowledge of the facts.

One truth children must understand in order to receive the Gospel is their sin nature. We need to help children understand that they have an internal sin nature, not just that they do wrong things. This is not something the natural man automatically understands.

In order to see their depravity and their subsequent need for the Gospel, children must understand the law's just demands. They must know the Ten Commandments and see their inability to live up to Jesus' standards of the attitudes of the heart in the Sermon on the Mount so they can understand grace. Ernest Reisinger writes in *Whatever Happened to the Ten Commandments?*,

> *In days gone by, children learned the commandments before they learned John 3:16, because only then did John 3:16 have real meaning for them. Likewise, John Eliot's first translation work among the Indians was not of John 3:16 but of the Ten Commandments, and he preached his first sermon on them. Did John Eliot think the Indians would be saved by the Ten Commandments? Of course not, but the Commandments would show them why they needed to be saved—they were law-breakers, and they needed a law-keeper to be their substitute.*[7]

God often, though not always, brings a preparatory work of the law to bear on the soul before bringing the soul to saving faith. We need to impress children over and over again with the holiness of God and the perfect obedience that God demands, and confront children with their inability to meet the law's demands—they need to see that their state is hopeless.

---

7. Reisinger, Ernest C. *Whatever Happened to the Ten Commandments?* (Edinburgh: The Banner of Truth Trust, 1999), 5.

Preparing the soil of a child's heart for the Gospel means helping a child to see and feel the holiness of God and the demand of perfect obedience. A big mistake that many Christian parents make is to jump too quickly to the Gospel without giving the child time to grasp the implications of God's holiness and his sin. However, the child needs time to see that choices have consequences—and he needs to feel those consequences. He needs to understand that punishment is an inevitable consequence of wrongdoing, and that hell is very real.

The Deciding Stage[8]

Age: seven to twelve years

Key Terms: conviction, struggle, faith, transformation

Our Role: caretaker—providing food for the new plant that it may grow

At this stage the child understands that the Gospel has implications for him personally—he must either make a personal commitment to Christ or reject the Savior. Saving faith involves surrendering our rebel hearts to God's control, and this often involves a battle that can be accompanied by emotional swings and attitude/behavioral problems. We do not see this battle in younger children, but this is because they are unable to count the cost of surrender; a 7-12 year old is more able to understand what is at stake in giving up control.

We can short-circuit this process if we presume that preschool spiritual interest is saving faith but this only prolongs the wait for the necessary spiritual battle to take place. However, it is better that rebellion against God is subdued when a person is young and the consequences are less severe than to wait until adulthood when the heart has been hardened by the deceitfulness of sin and the consequences are further reaching.

We need to purposefully walk with children through this stage, encouraging them to surrender to Jesus and place their trust in

---

8. Murphy, Art. *The Faith of a Child*. (Chicago: Moody Press, 2000), 63.

Him. Furthermore, we must remain dependent on the Holy Spirit to guide each child through this tumultuous stage.

This struggle is hard, but it is in this struggle that personal saving faith is experienced and transformation begins. Art Murphy articulates the importance of this struggle in his book *The Faith of a Child*, writing that,

> *During the deciding stages it is obvious that the child has moved from being curious to being convicted. He has chosen to have personal faith instead of depending on the faith of his parents or others. He now has a passion to please Christ instead of mere pleasantness from knowing what it means to be a Christian.*[9]

Remember that conversion does not always happen instantaneously but often involves a journey of questioning, evaluating, struggling, and learning to trust. Conversion is a process. The struggle is good—the ugliness of the human heart needs to be experienced and grieved over.

Often at this stage, our temptation as adults is to be impatient and jump to the resolution of the struggle—to "insure salvation for the child." Hence, this is where our faith as sowers is really tested: do we trust God to bring the child through victoriously? Will we trust in the sovereignty and goodness of God? It is at this time of waiting that our sin nature tempts us to take things into our own hands and push the child to make a commitment that he may be unprepared to make. We fear the outcome of the child's struggle and we want to secure the desired result. But we need to let go—to guide, encourage, point to Jesus by all means, but also to let go and let the child deal with God, and God with the child. We must not try to manipulate a response.

Sometimes this struggle can last for years, and it may be that we will not see immediate results from the truth we sow. But God calls us to be faithful sowers throughout the battle. One Reverend Edward Payson patiently guided his daughter through years of self-effort—all the time showing her error and the necessity of grace. Payson records Louisa's struggle to faith in the book *The*

---

9. Murphy, Art. *The Faith of a Child*. (Chicago: Moody Press, 2000), 63.

Pastor's Daughter. Her father understood that the message of the Gospel must be experienced not just told, and thus he was not afraid to let his daughter experience sorrow, heartache, anger, guilt, or shame. He guided her through years of trying to earn her salvation by "being good" enough to win God's favor—and confronted her over and over with her inadequacy. But her will was not easily broken, and the result of these years was as follows:

> *On the whole, the principal benefit she derived from all these years of trial and disappointment, was increased knowledge of the desperate wickedness of her heart, and a deeper conviction, that, of herself, she could never perform one holy act. These convictions did not, it is true, affect her heart, but they gained over her understanding and conscience to the side of truth.*[10]

Edward Payson allowed his daughter to reach a point of despair. He relentlessly confronted her with her need for a Savior; but he also kept holding out the grace of God to her. And then one day when her father was preaching on the love of Christ, Louisa (called Maria in the book) heard—and responded. This was the response with which God graciously gifted her:

> *Maria forgot herself, and her despondency; she thought only of the Savior who was thus presented to her; admiration, love, gratitude, and penitence filled her heart; and when her father said, that, if it were necessary to man's salvation, Christ would undergo all his sufferings again, a flood of tears burst from her eyes; she hid her face in her hands, and was ready to exclaim, "O, it is too much—too much! Such love to such a wretch!"*[11]

> *Instead of complaining that she could not "make her heart love God," she wondered how she could help loving him. Instead of thinking herself unfortunate in not being able to obey the commands of God, she*

---

10. Hopkins, Louisa Payson. *The Pastor's Daughter*. (Birmingham, Ala.: Solid Ground Christian Books, 2004), 136-137.
11. Ibid, 235.

perceived that it was entirely her own fault that she had not done so sooner.[12]

This is true conversion—worth years of struggle and turmoil.

The Discipling Stage[13]

Age: ten years and up

Key Terms: establishing habits, consistency, maturity, growing deeper, doctrine

Our Role: pruner—shaping, encouraging, the growing plant

This stage follows true conversion and is a period of growth in faith. The job of the sower does not end at this stage, but the sower's role changes in character and focus. Young faith must be directed and taught in the Word, have the life of faith modeled for it, and be sustained by prayer. The sower becomes a pruner as God shapes and brings faith into maturity.

The Fruit—Salvation and Evidences of Saving Faith

Conversion requires an understanding of the facts of the Gospel, turning away from unbelief and rebellion and turning to the Lord Jesus Christ in trust, surrender, and submission. The key elements involved in embracing the Gospel are repentance and faith.

As we have said, conversion is a process, not an event. Whether conversion culminates in "a prayer" or in a series of surrenderings leading to trust in Christ, eventually expressed in baptism, is probably not important. What is important is that a child be able to mark a time—a period or a season—when he turned to Jesus in faith.

---

12. Hopkins, Louisa Payson. *The Pastor's Daughter*. (Birmingham, Ala.: Solid Ground Christian Books, 2004), 236.
13. Murphy, Art. *The Faith of a Child*. (Chicago: Moody Press, 2000), 64.

True Repentance

As we look for evidences of saving faith, we need to understand what repentance is not and what it is. This is often what confuses children and adults about childhood experiences of tears and "turning from sin,"—it is easy to confuse worldly sorrow with true repentance.

We have all seen examples of worldly sorrow: an adult caught in moral failure who makes an apology and expects things to "return to normal." The husband who expects that an apology for infidelity should heal his relationship with his wife; a quickly whispered prayer for forgiveness for an act of disobedience. However, this is not the nature of repentance.

In *The Child's Book on Repentance*, Thomas Gallaudet examines the difference between worldly sorrow and true repentance. He explains that "If the only sorrow which you feel for having done what God forbids you to do, or for not having done what he commands you to do, is because you fear the punishment which he has threatened against those who break his laws, then you have no true repentance for your sins."[14] Instead, he writes,

> *True repentance is something more than a strong resolution or purpose that you will leave off sinning, and begin to love and obey God. Such a resolution will be of no use unless it proceeds from a heart-felt sorrow for your sins, as committed against a wise, holy, just and good God.*[15]

Gallaudet describes the truly repentant person as feeling,

> *[He] has done wrong in not rendering to God love and obedience. He feels that he has no excuse to make for not doing it. He feels that his own sinfulness and self-will have led him to refuse to do it. He acknowledges the great guilt of his pride and obstinacy of heart and is truly and deeply sorry for it. His will, subdued and humbled, bows in submission to the will of God; not as*

---

14. Gallaudet, Thomas H. *The Child's Book of Repentance* (Solid Ground Christian Books, 2005), 86.
15. Ibid, 86-87.

> *if forced to do it, as when a child yields to the will of the parent from the fear of punishment, but freely, fully and cheerfully desires to submit and trusts to Christ to aid him in doing it.*[16]

Gallaudet also points out that "you cannot truly repent of your sins without at the same time trusting entirely in Christ for the forgiveness of your sins, and your acceptance with God."[17]

Though we may not see the fullness of what Gallaudet describes as repentance, we should see the basic signs of repentance in a child who is desiring to trust Jesus: The child should feel that to sin is an offense against God, and that God's law is good. Furthermore, he should understand that he is unworthy of forgiveness and that the bent of his heart is to keep on sinning, and then desire cleansing from sin and a pure heart.

There are questions we should ask and answer when considering whether or not a child is ready to embrace Christ with true saving faith:

- Does he understand the Gospel? Can he articulate the Gospel and does he seem to understand the significance of it?
- Can he explain how a person is saved? Does he understand grace and has he seemed to abandon self-effort? Does he want to trust the work of Jesus on the cross for the forgiveness of his sins?
- Is there a conviction of sin?
- Does the child express affection for Jesus and a desire to follow Him?

---

16. Gallaudet, Thomas H. *The Child's Book of Repentance* (Solid Ground Christian Books, 2005), 90.
17. Ibid, 123.

True Conversion

How do we know if true conversion has taken place? In looking for evidence of true conversion, we need to contemplate the following questions:[18]

- Does the child have a present trust in Jesus? Note: "Believes" in John 3:16 is a present tense verb and should be interpreted as meaning "whoever continues believing in me."
- Is there a witness of the Holy Spirit in the child's heart? (Romans 8:15-16)
- Are there the fruits of the Spirit in the child's life? (Galatians 5:22; Matthew 7:16-20)
- Is there a pattern of spiritual growth in the child? Does he evidence continued spiritual interest, continued belief in Jesus, and growing sanctification? (2 Peter 1:5-10)

Concluding Thoughts

Obviously the stages set forth in this booklet are not absolute experiences in every child's life. Some people come to the Lord as adults, and there are those children who savingly trust in Jesus at a very young age. However, these stages are general parameters based on a child's developmental ability to comprehend and experience the elements of saving faith. While God is not bound to these stages, He very often works within the "limits" of His created order.

The danger we need to be wary of is assuming that a child is saved because he articulates a knowledge of God and the Gospel. John Piper remarked in a child's baptism class, "You can become a heretic by getting the facts wrong, and you can become a hypocrite by having fake experience." Whether the child gets the facts wrong or fakes the experience, he is lost.

At times, we may not know for sure whether faith is genuine or not. We can have a reasonable hope that a child may be truly

---

18. These questions are summarized from: Grudem, Wayne. *Systematic Theology* (Grand Rapids, Mich.: Zondervan, 1994), 803-806.

converted, but if we do not know, we should continue to present the truths of the Gospel—repentance and faith. We should continue to plead with the child to put his trust in Christ. This is the same message for believer and unbeliever alike: Believe on Christ! It is a message that encourages the unbeliever to repent and come to saving faith, and encourages believers to persevere in faith.

In the Parable of the Weeds (Matthew 13:24-30), Jesus speaks of a wheat field that becomes infested with weeds. For a time, the farmer allows the weeds and the wheat to grow up together. However, at harvest time, the farmer instructs the reapers to separate the two. They are then to burn the weeds, and gather the wheat into the barn. The same gathering and separating will happen one day in the church. As Jesus says, "Every plant that my heavenly Father has not planted will be rooted up" (Matthew 15:13).

We do have hypocrites among the children of our churches. For those who think they are saved but show no evidence of saving faith, we need to lovingly discern whether there are evidences of saving faith and challenge them to examine their hearts and lives. We have deprived many children of real struggle—the kind of struggle that leads to conversion.

If they belong to Christ, He will faithfully bring that struggle into their lives in order to bring them to Himself. The salvation of children (of everyone) is ultimately the work of God, and while we sow and plant, God will be the one who gives the growth (1 Corinthians 3:4-9). It is in His power to save that we are to find our hope.

Part Two: Presenting the Gospel to Children

Imagine a family going for a boat ride on a beautiful summer day on Lake Superior. Being the careful parents that they are, each child is wearing a new life jacket, the best that money can buy. The kids love the jackets because they have neat child-friendly designs and colors. The children are now safe in the unlikely event that the boat should sink or be overwhelmed by waves. But there is something that the parents and children have not taken into account. Lake Superior is very cold. Even in the summer, the water temperature hovers around 55° F. So as wonderful as those life jackets may seem, and as much as the parents and children feel safe in the event of the boat being overwhelmed, the real danger remains unforeseen and unplanned for —hypothermia. In the event that the family is tossed into the water and is left to float, eventually the frigid temperature of the water will kill them.

The Gospel Man Has Created

Unfortunately, the "gospel" that we often present to children is like those life jackets. It is a gospel that we think will protect and save our children, but it is not the safety assurance that we envision it to be. And it may be that while our children think they are safely bound for eternal life in heaven, in reality they continue their slow but dangerous "float" in the deadly waters of hell. Why is this so? Because it is not the Gospel of Scripture.

How have we changed the true life-saving Gospel into a child-friendly and colorful but ineffective type of life jacket? Here are a few characteristics of this changed gospel and why it is so deadly:

This changed gospel puts man at its center instead of God. It presents a plan instead of a Person. It seeks to comfort but not convict. It calls for acceptance of Christ but not repentance. It encourages acknowledging true facts rather than embracing and submitting to the One who is both Savior and Lord. It enslaves men to works instead of freeing them to do good works.

But that is not all this "gospel" states. It claims to save by man's decisive choice instead of God's sovereign grace. It promises affirmation instead of radical transformation. It exalts man and the desire to be loved instead of exalting God's love displayed in the person and work of Jesus Christ, who alone brings us near to God so that we might experience the immeasurable joy of making much of Him.

This man-created and skewed gospel is not good news!

The Gospel That Saves

So what is the true Gospel, and how do we present it in a way that can be clearly understood and embraced by children so that they may be saved? To begin with, there are three foundational themes we must understand:

First, GOD is the starting point of the Gospel. The message of the Gospel begins with God. He is the source of the Gospel—it was His sovereign plan from all eternity (2 Timothy 1:8-10). When we present the Gospel to children we need to start with God, not with ourselves. He is both the founder and the foundation of the message.

Second, GOD is the vehicle of the Gospel. He Himself is the means by which the Gospel happens and is accomplished. Too many times children are presented with a Gospel that gives them the impression that it is ultimately their worth or their own decision that saves them—but this is not the case. The central message and means of saving faith is focused on the Person and work of God's Son, Jesus—His worth, demonstrated in His perfect obedience, His substitutionary death and His glorious resurrection (1 Corinthians 15:1-4). Even saving faith is ultimately brought about by God's decisive act in the human heart—it is a gift from Him, so that no one can boast (Ephesians 2:1-9).

Finally, GOD is the goal of the Gospel. Heaven is not the ultimate goal. Sin forgiven is not the ultimate goal. Our happiness is not the ultimate goal of the Gospel. God is the goal: that His greatness and worth would be treasured most of all (Philippians 3:7-8,

1 Peter 2:9). The Gospel exists to bring us near to God so that we might trust, love, treasure, enjoy, and worship Him forever. And yes, that God-centered and God-exalting goal does result in our ultimate and everlasting joy! (Psalm 16:11).

Presenting the Gospel: In Context

Keeping these three foundational themes in mind can now help us in determining what key elements of the Gospel must be presented, as well as the manner in which we present them. The starting of the Gospel message is the text of the Bible itself. To be faithful to the Gospel, we must understand the text and the context of the message—namely, the whole counsel of God. Sometimes people believe that the Gospel is just found in the writings of the New Testament. However, the foundation of the Gospel is rooted in the Old Testament. The Old Testament, as it were, is the tree that grew and supplied the wood from which the cross of the Jesus was cut. As Paul writes to Timothy in 2 Timothy 3:14-15,

> *"But as for you, continue in what you have learned and have firmly believed, knowing from whom you learned it and how from childhood you have been acquainted with the sacred writings, which are able to make you wise for salvation through faith in Christ Jesus."*

According to Paul, the Gospel message included the teaching of the Old Testament as it serves to make us "wise for salvation." The whole purpose of the Old Testament is to set the stage for the unveiling of the good news of Jesus. It reveals the character of God and the desperate condition of sinful men, and then foreshadows and points the way to Jesus. The Old Testament demonstrates why the Gospel of Jesus is such good news!

Presenting the Gospel: With Intentionality

Thus, to present the Gospel in a manner that truthfully and accurately explains this life-saving good news in a God-centered manner within its proper context, we must be intentional in our approach. What are the essential elements of the Gospel that our children must know, understand, and embrace? And how can they be presented in a manner that is not only biblically accurate but also understandable for children?

Clearly this task is not a one-time, 15-minute presentation. Rather, we are suggesting using a progressive presentation of 10 essential Gospel truths. This is the method outlined in the family devotional guide found later in this booklet. Ideally, these truths would be presented slowly over a period of time and then be repeated and explained further as the children grow and mature. There are four parts to each devotional as it presents one essential Gospel truth: Scripture, Explanation, Illustration, and Implication.

Scripture

Each devotional will begin with a suggested verse (or verses) that support the specific Gospel truth presented in the session. Please note that this is not a comprehensive list of supporting Scripture passages. Rather, the key verse is carefully chosen to convey key Gospel truths and yet be simple enough to explain to children.

Explanation

This involves explaining the key truth in a way that is understandable to children. Often people have tended to change the Gospel message for children instead of simply explaining the message. But this is dangerous. That is why the Scriptures texts given are key. Don't *change* these truths—*explain* them. However, also avoid "over-explaining" concepts, especially with younger children. Keep the explanation as simple as possible. You are laying a foundation that you will continue to build on in the future. As the children grow and mature, so will the explanation and discussion.

Be sure to focus on explaining key Bible words and doctrines. Often as adults, we use terms such as "eternal" or "sovereign" or "sin" or "hell," and we take it for granted that children understand what we mean. Along with this, be very careful about how you define words. For example, do not define "sin" as "mistakes." This could give rise to misinterpretation and confusion. Children often think of mistakes as unintentional things they do. For example: "I spilled my milk by mistake." "I put on the wrong colored sock by mistake." Sins are not mistakes. Sin is rebellion against God. Sin is saying to your sovereign Ruler: "I will decide what is true and right—not You."

Finally, remember that young children are information gatherers. They are much more willing than adults to accept truth without questioning it, which is why it is so important to impart biblical truth at a young age. It is acceptable to make statements of fact without pursuing a complicated discussion on the topic. Included in the devotionals are deep and somewhat abstract truths that young children may not fully understand at this point. However, the children still need to be hear those truths over and over again. As they grow and become more abstract thinkers, they will begin to more fully comprehend the meaning of those truths.

Illustration

This involves demonstrating truth through concrete visuals, life experiences, etc. However, while these illustrations may serve to demonstrate truths in a more concrete manner, they should not be used as direct comparisons to biblical truth. When illustrations are used, end by saying something such as, *"This can help us to understand what it means that..."* This will help the children separate the limited analogy from the biblical truth.

Implication

The key truths presented in these devotionals are not a collection of impersonal information for us and our children to simply know and acknowledge. These biblical truths have personal implications for each of us as they challenge—even demand— that the mind, heart, and will respond. The Gospel message is a personal message to every person, and every person must respond to it.

Presenting the Gospel: At Every Opportunity, With Prayer

Embracing the Gospel is not simply a one-time decision. The truths of the Gospel should embrace all of life. We must therefore teach the Gospel diligently—when we sit at home or walk along the way, lie down, or rise (Deuteronomy 6:7). Always look for opportunities to share these truths. For example, maybe your children have just learned about David and his sin concerning Uriah. Use that as an opportunity to share the truth that all people are desperate sinners, even the Bible hero, King David. Just like us, King David needed God's mercy. Just like us, King David needed a Savior. God placed the punishment that David deserved on Jesus.

After the Gospel truths are presented, pray for and with your child about their response to the Gospel. Try to discern the difference between whether they are expressing general spiritual curiosity, or true repentance and belief. Yes, we want encourage the children to "say a prayer," but be careful not to manipulate and pressure them into responses that they neither understand nor genuinely embrace

Ultimately, saving faith is not determined by our presentation of the message, or the manner in which we present it. We are called to be faithful and "acquaint" our children with the sacred writings, but it is God alone who brings about saving faith. We can prepare the soil of a child's heart. We can plant the seed of the Gospel. We can water the Gospel by explaining and reviewing its amazing truths. But that Gospel seed will lie dormant in the heart of a child until God, if He wills it, by the power of the Holy Spirit causes that seed to burst forth into newness of life.

Part Three: Family Devotionals— Ten Essential Truths of the Gospel

How to Use this Devotional Guide

Prepare before you present
Look over the devotional before you present it. Each devotional has a listing of helpful hints that may aid you when you are presenting.

Set your own pace
Please do not feel the pressure to add more information than is here, but please do not resist fruitful avenues of discussion beyond this guide either.

Dwell on each truth
This is a progressive presentation meant to be completed over time, purposefully and slowly. You are encouraged to meditate on each truth for an appropriate season of time (we recommend one week).

Follow the order
This devotional is as succinct as possible and is purposeful in its order. Therefore, simply begin with "what is true" and end with "what this means."

Pray for help
Pray that God would give understanding and that His Spirit would awaken your child's heart to embrace His truth.

Bless your family
Close your time together by praying the "Blessing for Truth" over your child and family.

Look for opportunities
Look for teachable moments through the week to apply these truths to your child's life.

Gospel Devotional: Truth One

1) **Truth One**
   God is the sovereign Creator of all things.

2) **Scripture**
   Psalm 19:1; Psalm 22:28; Psalm 24:1; Isaiah 44:24

   Read these passages of Scripture, as well as any other Scripture that supports the truth that God is the sovereign Creator of all things.

3) **Explanation**
   There is one living, eternal God who created all things. Eternal means God had no beginning and will have no ending. God was never born; He never had a birthday. He has always been alive and will always be alive. God will never die.

   This one, eternal God made everything—all by Himself. God made the sky, stars, ground, trees, plants, animals, and all the people. God can do this because He is an almighty God. This means God is all-powerful and that nothing is too hard for Him to do.

   Because God made everything, everything belongs to God. God owns all of the rocks, trees, stars, oceans, plants, and people—everything! God is also the sovereign ruler over all He has created. That means God is "the boss." He is in charge. He is the King of His creation, and He controls it and rules over it.

4) **Illustration**
   a) *Pay attention*
   God has created all things, and when we pay attention to what He has made, we can learn some things about God by looking at what He created.

   Ask: Have you seen a rainbow? It is beautiful. God made it, and God is beautiful. Have you heard thunder? It is powerful. God made it, and God is powerful. What is your favorite food? It tastes so good. God made it, and God is good. Isn't it great to get a hug from someone you love, like your parents who love you? God is love, and He loves you. Puppies are the happiest little animals, aren't they? God made them, and He is the happiest being in the universe.

   b) *It is a crazy idea*

   Take some crayons and paper, and draw an animal (you decide as a family what animal to draw). Each person may do this, or just one for the family. Finish drawing, and then ask the following questions:

   What if the crayons said, "We don't want to draw a puppy"? Should the crayons decide what the picture will be, or the one who is drawing? It is a crazy idea to think the crayons should decide.

   Just as it would be crazy for the crayons to decide what is drawn, it would be foolish for us to believe that we can think or do whatever we want. God is in charge of everything, and everything belongs to God—including us. He made all things, and it is His right alone to decide what is made and how it is made.

5) Implication

God made you. You belong to God. God is your ruler.

Additional Helps: Truth One

Additional Reading

The following texts are designed to assist the devotional guide by providing you additional opportunities to review this truth throughout the week.

Other helpful texts: Genesis 1-2:3; Job 38; Psalm 19:1-6; Psalm 24; Isaiah 40:12-26

Prayer Prompts

- Read Psalm 19:1-6: The heavens, bigger than us, were made by One bigger than them!

- What might it look like for you to honor God as sovereign in the normal routines of your life as a family? What would it look like to honor God as sovereign when you go to school or work, or just wash the dishes?

- God reigns over your lives, even in hard, frustrating times. Every circumstance is governed by the good, sovereign God.

- How might you honor God as Creator when looking at creation? Think of those times creation is all around you but you don't take notice of its message—like when you are driving in the car (sky, trees, birds, clouds, etc.). How can you change your noticing habits?

A Prayer of Blessing for Truth One

> "May you be numbered with those who wonder in awe at the greatness of God
>
> For He made all things
>
> He alone stretched out the heavens
>
> He alone spread out the earth by Himself
>
> The earth is the LORD's and all that is in it
>
> May you declare God's glory, as the heavens do
>
> Kingship belongs to the LORD and He rules over the nations
>
> He rules over you; May you delight in His rule
>
> Indeed, may you be numbered with those who wonder in awe at the greatness of God"

A Word for Parents

Nan Gurley's book *Twice Yours*[19] captures your heart with the truth of the Gospel. It is a children's picture book that presents Gospel truth in the depicting a grandfather and a grandson. This is, in simple terms, "a keeper" as there are few like it.

> *Grandpa finished the story and whittled the last piece from his block of wood. Then he handed the carving to Cory. It was a cross. "This is for you, Cory. It will remind you of the One who made you and then bought you."*

---

19. Gurley, Nan. Illustrated by Bill Farnsworth. *Twice Yours*. (Grand Rapids, Mich.: Zonderkidz, 2001).

Gospel Devotional: Truth Two

1) Review Previous Truth

Truth One: God is the sovereign Creator of all things.

2) Truth Two

God created people for His glory.

3) Scripture

Psalm 29:1-2; Isaiah 43:6-7; 1 Corinthians 10:31

Read these passages of Scripture as well as any other Scripture that you know of that support the truth that God created people for His glory.

4) Explanation

People make things to have a special purpose. For example, cars are made for driving; refrigerators are made to keep food cold. These things are made in a special way so they can do what they were made to do.

God created people for a special purpose also, so God created people in a certain way. God created men and women and boys and girls in His image and likeness. That means God created people to be like Him in certain ways. God created us different from the animals and all other things. For example, we were created with minds that can learn about God. Dogs cannot learn about God. God created us with hearts that have certain feelings and emotions so we could love God. Giraffes cannot know and love God in the way that we can.

Why did God make people in His image and likeness? God made us this way so we would show how great He is! God created us so we could know Him and have a very special kind of relationship with Him. God wants us to know and love Him so you and I would want to say: *God is the greatest and best! I love Him most of all! God makes me happier than anything or anyone else!* This is the purpose God created you for!

God wants His people to be able to know and love Him forever. That is why God created heaven. Heaven is a place for God's people to live with Him forever. Living forever with God is the best thing ever!

5) **Illustration**

   a) *Reflecting God's greatness*

   If possible, do this illustration after dark.

   Turn off the lights in the house. Then, shine a flashlight on a mirror and aim the mirror anywhere in the room. Ask, do you see the light shine through the reflection? As you turn the mirror, the light shines in different places.

   You have been created to be like a mirror that reflects or shows back that God is great and wonderful. We do this by gladly trusting, loving, and serving God.

   b) *Real vs. Like*

   Collect some toy trucks and/or a stuffed bear. Use them as examples during the following discussion.

Are toy trucks real trucks? No. However, they are like real trucks in some ways. So it is with people and God. We are not God, but we were made to show what God is like.

Is a stuffed bear a real bear? No. However, it is like a real bear in some ways. So it is with people and God. We are not God, but we were made to show what God is like.

c) *Holidays and Heaven*

Talk about a good time you have had as a family (holiday, vacation, etc). That was great, wasn't it? Then explain that living with God is so much better—living with God in heaven will be more wonderful than anything you could ever imagine!

d) *Made in God's image*

Discuss how we as people are made in God's image. Animals do not have this special privilege. Ask the following questions.

Can dogs pray? No. Can dogs sing songs of praise to God like people do? No. Can dogs open up the Bible and read about God? No. Can dogs know and obey God like we do? No.

Discuss other ways people express their uniqueness as God's image bearers.

6) Implication

God created you to know, trust, and love Him most of all.

Additional Helps: Truth Two

Additional Reading

Read about John's vision in Revelation 4:8-1; 5:1-14; 19:6-10. Notice all the glory God is receiving from His created beings.

Prayer Prompts

- Read Isaiah 43:6-7. God is drawing to Himself people who were made to give Him glory. Can you imagine a multitude of people so great that you cannot count them? Can you imagine them all praising and serving God perfectly, without sin? This is what it will be like in heaven for God's people. Do you long for heaven?

- Do you know of anyone close to you who is not interested in bringing God the glory He deserves? Pray for him.

A Prayer of Blessing for Truth Two

> "May you bring God glory, and for the honor of His great name tell of His greatness
>
> For He is the One who said
>
> > "I will say to the north, 'give up'
> >
> > And to the south, 'do not withhold
> >
> > Bring my sons from afar and my daughters from the ends of the earth
> >
> > Everyone who is called by My name
> >
> > Whom I have created for My glory; Whom I formed and made'"
>
> God has formed you and made you for His glory
>
> May you follow His design for your life by living for Him

*May you honor the name of the One who created you;
the mighty name of God*

Therefore, whether you eat or drink or whatever you do

*May you bring God glory, and for the honor of His name
tell of His greatness"*

A Word for Parents

John Piper's book *Desiring God*[20] captures many lofty concepts, one being our call to glorify God by enjoying Him forever. This is what we were created for. *Desiring God* is one of those books to be read and re-read. This is a work that requires effort to comprehend, so take your time as it is worth the effort and it helps illuminate the foundation of our faith.

> *Worship will happen when the God who said, "Let light shine out of darkness," shines in our hearts to give us "the light of the knowledge of the glory of God in the face of Christ" (2 Corinthians 4:6). We must see and feel the incomparable excellency of the Son of God. Incomparable because in him meet infinite glory and lowest humility, infinite majesty and transcendent meekness, deepest reverence toward God and equality with God, infinite worthiness of good and greatest patience to suffer evil, supreme dominion and exceeding obedience, divine self-sufficiency and childlike trust.*

Gospel Devotional: Truth Three

1) Review Previous Truths

Truth One: God is the sovereign Creator of all things.

Truth Two: God created people for His glory.

---

20. Piper, John. *Desiring God*. (Sisters, Ore.: Multnomah Books, 1986), 94.

2) Truth Three

God is holy and righteous.

3) Scripture

Leviticus 19:2, 37; Deuteronomy 32:4; Romans 7:12

Read these passages of Scripture as well as any other Scripture that you know of that support the truth that God is holy and righteous.

4) Explanation

God is so great He is unlike anyone or anything else. God is holy. That means God is perfect in every way. God is also righteous—everything He thinks, says, and does is right. He never does anything wrong. God has never sinned and never will sin.

Because God is holy and righteous, and because God made you and me to be like Him, we must be holy and righteous, too. In the Bible, God gave us His holy and righteous commands. They are good commands. For example: the Ten Commandments tell us what kind of thoughts, desires, words, and actions are holy and righteous. To be holy and righteous, God says people must obey these commands, perfectly, all of the time.

5) Illustration

a) Rules

Use toy cars as an illustration. Talk about the cars for just a minute or so. What kind of car would you like to drive? When you are done, follow this question with discussion.

Would it be okay for a four-year-old girl or boy to get into a car and drive? No. It would not be safe for the boy or girl, or others. It is a good rule that keeps little children from driving cars.

Talk about the kinds of rules that are in place at home, such having as a young child hold her father's hand when crossing the street. How many rules can you come up with? These rules show that daddy and mommy love you and want to protect you. They are good rules. Talk about rules from our government that are designed for our good and protection. God's rules are even better. God's rules are the best!

You might consider looking up the Ten Commandments (Exodus 20:1-17). Discuss how each command is perfect and right and good.

6) Implication

God is holy and righteous. God's commands are holy and righteous. You must obey God's commands all the time.

Additional Helps: Truth Three

Additional Reading

Read the story about Hannah in 1 Samuel 1-2:2 and notice her final words in 2:2. Also read Deuteronomy 31:30-32:4 and Isaiah 6:1-4.

Prayer Prompts

- Read Deuteronomy 32:1-4. God is just, faithful and without any sin. Pause in silence for just a moment to think about this truth. You might consider re-reading verse 4.

- Consider God. He is perfectly holy and righteous, and He justly demands perfect holiness and righteousness from us. We really do not comprehend the weight of God's holiness. Ask Him for a spiritual sense of this truth.

- Read Isaiah 6:1-4. Did you know that the word "holy" is the only word used three times in a row in the Bible to describe God? This was done to emphasize its importance!

A Prayer of Blessing for Truth Three

"May you think rightly about God, knowing who He is

> *He is holy, holy, holy*
>
> *He is perfect and His ways are perfect*
>
> *He is faithful and just*

May you think rightly about God's law and what He requires from all people

> *He requires holiness from all people*
>
> *His law is holy and righteous and good*

Yes, may you think rightly about God and about what He requires from all people"

A Word for Parents

A. W. Tozer's book *The Knowledge of the Holy*[21] is a short but moving work designed to move us to worship God in the truth of who He is. A. W. Tozer calls us to see God for who He is and the result of this shows us for who we are thus pointing us to the only place for hope: Jesus.

> *I believe there is scarcely an error in doctrine or a failure in applying Christian ethics that cannot be traced finally to imperfect and ignoble thoughts about God...All the problems of heaven and earth, though they were to confront us together and at once, would be nothing compared with the overwhelming problem of God: That He is; what He is like; and what we as moral beings must do about Him.*

Gospel Devotional: Truth Four

1) Review Previous Truths

Truth One: God is the sovereign Creator of all things.

Truth Two: God created people for His glory.

Truth Three: God is holy and righteous.

2) Truth Four

Man is sinful.

3) Scripture

Romans 3:10-18, 20, 23

---

21. Tozer, A. W. *The Knowledge of the Holy.* (San Francisco: Harper Collins Publishers, 1962), 2-3.

Read these passages of Scripture as well as any other Scripture that you know of that supports the truth that man is sinful.

4) Explanation

In the Bible, God's laws—including the Ten Commandments—show us God is holy and righteous. And because God is holy and righteous, God's people must also be holy and righteous. If we are to live with God in heaven forever, we must obey all His commands perfectly, all the time. We must never do anything wrong. Can we do this? Have you ever disobeyed any of God's commands? Which ones? Have I?

So God's commands also show us something else: they show us that we are not holy and righteous. God's commands show us we do not obey God all the time. God's commands show us we all break His laws. That means everyone—all people, even children and babies—are sinners. Being a sinner is the opposite of being holy and righteous. Sin is disobeying God. When did our sin begin? We were born with sin. From the very first moment you started growing inside your mommy's body, you had a sin nature; the desire to sin (Psalm 51:5). When a little baby gets angry and arches his back because dad is putting him in his car seat, he is acting out his sin nature. When a little toddler stamps her foot and says, "NO!" to mom, she is acting out her sin nature.

We received our sin nature from the first man, Adam, when he sinned in the Garden of Eden. We show we are sinners like him by the wrong things we think, desire, say and do. For example, we do not always love God most of all. We do not obey His good command to honor mom and dad. Sometimes we lie about something we did and want to hide.

5) Illustration

a) The two mirrors

Find two mirrors, any size. Make one dirty so that you cannot see your reflection. Keep the other one clean.

Take the clean mirror and place something beautiful from God's creation (e.g., flower) in front of it. Ask, does the mirror reflect or show [the flower] clearly? Yes. That is what mirrors are made to do. This can help us to understand what God created us to do: we are to be like mirrors that reflect or show how beautiful and wonderful God is.

Take the dirty mirror and place the [flower] in front of it. Ask, can you see the reflection of the [flower] clearly? No. Why not? What has changed? The flower or the mirror?

The mirror changed and it is not doing what it is supposed to do. It is "falling short" of doing what it was made to do. This is like us. We are sinners and our hearts are darkened (Romans 1:21). Because of this, we are not able to do what God created us to do. Our sin prevents us from reflecting or showing to God that He is holy and righteous. We prove this to be true as we do not perfectly obey God's commands.

b) Instinct

> Ask the following questions: If I gave a lion a head of lettuce and a big piece of raw meat, which one do you think he would eat? The meat! How about if I gave a rabbit a carrot and a piece of fish, which one do you think he would eat? The carrot!
>
> The lion and the rabbit both have a built-in or "inborn" desire for a certain kind of food. We, too, have a built-in or "inborn" desire. Our inborn desire is for sin. Just like a lion is born with the desire for meat, we are born with the desire to sin against God.

6) Implications

> You have disobeyed God's commands. You are a sinner.

Additional Helps: Truth Four

Additional Reading

Read these three stories about the sinfulness of man in Genesis 3:1-7; 6:1-7; Daniel 5:1-23. Also read Isaiah 1:2-4, 12-15; 59:1-3; Romans 3:10-18, 20, 23; I John 1:8.

Prayer Prompts

- Read Romans 3:10-12, 20, 23 . Allow it to instruct your time in prayer. These may be familiar words, but do we have a spiritual sense of what they mean? Ask for a sense of what this means.

- The psalmist said in Psalm 119:128 he hated every false way. Pray for this hatred of sin to be true of your heart as well.

- How would you define sin? Sin is falling "short" of the glory of God—not treasuring Him most of all, disobeying His perfect commands, exchanging the honor and thanks due Him to other things.

A Prayer of Blessing for Truth Four

> "May you think rightly about yourself as your thinking is guided by God's Word
>
> > There is none righteous in God's eyes
> >
> > There is no one who seeks after God
> >
> > There is no one who does good—no, not even one
>
> If you say you have no sin, you deceive yourself
>
> May you agree with your head and heart about what God says: man is sinful
>
> May God use this right thinking for His purposes in your heart: His purposes are good"

A Word for Parents

Jeremiah Burroughs' book *The Evil of Evils*[22] is a very weighty book concerning sin. He is a Puritan, so you need to work hard at times to read his work. However, it is worth it. He has a way of shaking readers to make a point, and concerning this topic his approach is most appropriate.

> *How does sin wrong God? The wrong you do to God by sin is such wrong that, if all the angels in heaven and all the men in the world would be content to endure thousands of years of torments in hell to make up that wrong, it could not be done. Any one sin that you commit does such wrong to God...Sin makes this*

---
22. Burroughs, Jeremiah. *The Evil of Evils.* (first published in 1654) (Morgan, Penn: Soli Deo Gloria Publications, 1992), 45.

profession, that there is not enough good in God to satisfy this soul.

Gospel Devotional: Truth Five

1) Review Previous Truths

Truth One: God is the sovereign Creator of all things.

Truth Two: God created people for His glory.

Truth Three: God is holy and righteous.

Truth Four: Man is sinful.

2) Truth Five

God is just and is right to punish sin.

3) Scripture

Isaiah 59:2; Romans 1:18; Romans 6:23a (note: read only the first part of Romans 6:23 at this time: "The wages of sin is death.")

Read these passages of Scripture as well as any other Scripture that you know of that supports the truth that God is just and right to punish sin.

4) Explanation

Because God is holy and righteous, He is right to not permit or allow any sin. Sin, even one sin, is not "okay" with God. God hates sin and is very angry with sin. God is right to punish sin. That is what it means that God is "just." God has decided the right punishment for sin is death and hell. Hell is a place where sinners will experience God's great anger forever.

Because everyone is a sinner, including you and me, we all deserve to be punished by God. God would be right and just to send us all to hell. Is there anything we can do to help ourselves? We cannot become sinless by trying to do more good things than bad things. It's too late for that, isn't it? We have already sinned too many times. We cannot obey God perfectly, no matter how hard we work at it. We have a sin nature that makes us like the wrong things and makes us want to do the wrong things. We cannot clean away our sin. There is nothing we can do to help ourselves. Not even mom and dad cannot help you. Mom and dad are helpless sinners too.

There is nothing more terrible than hell. It is worse than spankings or discipline, or being afraid or being apart from mom and dad forever. We can never be happy in hell, but we are helpless to save ourselves from going to hell. We can only be happy forever if we go to heaven and live with God forever, but sinners cannot go to heaven. We deserve to be sent to hell. This is a huge problem—this is your biggest problem!

(Note: Parents, do not worry about your children feeling bad about sin. There is not one of us who feels as bad as we should. Feeling a deep sorrow for sin is a very important part of true repentance. You need to feel something of the depth of our condemnation before a holy God before you can begin to truly be amazed by the free gift of justification.)

5) Illustration

a) Jail/Prison

Ask, why do we have prisons and why are they full of people? Because people commit crimes—sin—and they need to be punished. Can you imagine if there was no punishment for doing wrong? Why is it right for guilty people to be punished? What should it show us?

b) Cookies

Help your children make a batch of cookies and have the following discussion: Suppose you decide not to follow the instructions on the recipe—change one little thing: bake the cookies for 30 minutes instead of 10 minutes. What do the cookies look and taste like after 30 minutes? Can they take these burnt cookies and make them "unburnt"? Why not? What would the right thing be to do with these cookies? Why?

When we disobey even one of God's commands it is a little bit like baking the cookies the wrong way—just as the cookies become darkened and bad, our hearts have become darkened with sin. And just like we would not say, "It's okay not to follow the instructions. These cookies are great anyway," God will not say, "I was just kidding when I said you must obey Me. I won't really punish you with death and hell. You are okay just as you are." Just like we are helpless to change these cookies, we are helpless to change our sinful hearts. As sinners, we are even more worthless than these burnt cookies and we deserve something much, much worse than being thrown in the garbage. We deserve death and hell.

6) Implication

You deserve God's punishment of death and hell. You are helpless to save yourself.

Additional Helps: Truth Five

Additional Reading

Read 1 Samuel 13:1-15, a story to help explain that man sins and God is right to punish. Read Psalm 100 and consider that all our good comes from God for He is good, and yet we still sin. Read also Romans 1:18-32 and 1 Thessalonians 1:8-9.

Prayer Prompts

- Why is God right to punish sin? Talk about it; then tell Him in prayer.

- Read Psalm 100. Quietly consider the goodness of God. Next, quietly consider the sinfulness of man against God's goodness. Then, ask God for a sense of what all of this really means as you pray.

A Prayer of Blessing for Truth Five

"*May you see clearly the truth about who God is*

   He is holy

   He is just and right to punish sin

May you be blessed with eyes to see

May you be blessed with a tender heart that feels

   May you grieve sin

   May you hate sin

May you feel desperate to get rid of sin

May you be quick to tell the truth: God is just and right to punish sin

May God do as He pleases in your heart, as you think about these things"

A Word for Parents

C.J. Mahaney's book *Christ Our Mediator*[23] is succinct, clear, moving, and full of Gospel truth. Our personal libraries should not only include long deep works on Jesus, but also short works that are instantly penetrating. This is such a work—short and powerful, and perhaps even accessible to your children under your teaching and care. Read anything by C.J. Mahaney; he is a man who understands grace more than most people.

> *Let me ask you: With whom do you most identify in the events of this dark day (the cross)...Let me tell you who I identify with. I identity most with the angry mob screaming, "Crucify Him!" That's who we should all identify with. Because apart from God's grace, this is where we would all be standing, and we're only flattering ourselves to think otherwise. Unless you see yourself standing there with the shrieking crowd, full of hostility and hatred for the holy and innocent Lamb of God, you don't really understand the nature and depth of your sin or the necessity of the cross.*

Gospel Devotional: Truth Six

1) Review Previous Truths

Truth One: God is the sovereign Creator of all things.

Truth Two: God created people for His glory.

Truth Three: God is holy and righteous.

---

23. Mahaney, C.J. *Christ Our Mediator*. (Sisters, Ore.: Multnomah Publishers, 2004), 65-66.

Truth Four: Man is sinful.

Truth Five: God is just and is right to punish sin.

2) Truth Six
God is merciful. He is kind to undeserving sinners.

3) Scripture
Psalm 145:8; Ephesians 2:8-9

Read these passages of Scripture as well as any other Scripture that you know of that supports the truth that God is merciful—He is kind to undeserving sinners.

4) Explanation
God is holy and righteous, and He is right to demand that people be holy and righteous like Him. God's commands show us what it means to be holy and righteous. God's commands also show us that we are all sinners. Because God is just, He is right to punish sinners, you and me, with death and hell. This is our biggest problem! We are helpless to solve this problem. Is there anyone who could help us? Yes. God can help us solve this problem! God is all-powerful and nothing is too hard for Him to do.

Why would He want to help us? Because God is a merciful God. That means that God is kind to sinners who do not deserve His kindness. God's mercy and grace is like a free gift or present. Presents are wonderful things someone gives to you which you do not deserve. God gives helpless sinners the free gift of His kindness. It is a free gift from God because it is not something you deserve. God gives it to sinners because He wants to, not because He owes it to anyone. You cannot work for God's mercy or earn God's mercy by anything you do.

How does God show He is merciful to sinners? One way God is merciful is by being patient with us. Even though God is right to be very angry with sin, God is slow to get angry and slow to punish us. God does not have a temper tantrum when people sin. God's anger is not "out of control." He does not instantly throw us into hell when we sin. The fact that you and I are still alive even after we have sinned against God proves God is patient with us. This is a free gift of His kindness to us—even though we do not deserve His kindness.

Even though God is patient, He still must punish sin because He is a just and righteous God. So God, in His mercy, made a way for sin to be punished and for sinners be saved. God, in His great kindness, made a way for sinners to be saved from death and hell so we could go to heaven and live forever with God. That is the most merciful thing God could do! That is the best free gift God could ever give to sinners. Did God have to do this? No. God did this because He is merciful—He is kind to undeserving sinners.

5) **Illustration**

   a) *Surprise Gift*
   Surprise your child with by giving him $1.00. Ask him if it was something he earned. No; it was a gift. Why did you give him $1.00? Just because of your love for your child; it is an expression of kindness—mercy. This is a little bit like God's mercy—an undeserved gift that He gives to sinners.

b) *Impossible Task*
Give your child an impossible task to do in the morning, something that is outside of her ability to do by herself, like moving the sofa. Promise her $1.00 when it is done. Let her try to do it all day long. At the end of the day, have dad do the task, but give the $1.00 to your child anyway.

Ask your child if she earned the $1.00. No, it was a gift because she didn't do the job. Then why was it given to her? Just because of your love for your child; it is an expression of kindness—mercy. This is a little bit like God's mercy. It is impossible for us to be saved through our own efforts. But just as dad stepped in and did what you could not do, God, in His mercy, made a way for helpless sinners to be saved.

6) Implication
You must depend on God's mercy in order to be saved.

Additional Helps: Truth Six

Additional Reading

Read Genesis 3. God did punish Adam and Eve, but He was merciful and did not take their lives immediately. He also promised a deliverer; what a mercy indeed! Read also Psalm 28:1-2, 6; Luke 15:11-32; and 1 Timothy 1:12-17.

Prayer Prompts

Perhaps a good way to pray would be to read through the story of the Prodigal Son (Luke 15:11-32). Notice the kind heart of the father, not only to one son but to the other as well. God is merciful. May this story instruct you in the way you should pray.

A Prayer of Blessing for Truth Six

> "May God bless you with great expressions of His mercy, of His kindness
>
> May He visit you with love, even though you have done nothing to earn it
>
> May you be like the Prodigal
>
>> May you turn and face your heavenly Father
>>
>> May you seek His face and seek His mercy
>>
>>> For His kindness is real, but beyond comprehension
>
> May He look upon you with mercy, kindness, gentleness and compassion
>
> May you know the mercy of God, both now and forever"

A Word for Parents

Altogether Lovely[24] is a book that contains a number of sermons by Jonathan Edwards on the excellencies of Christ. This is one of those books that should not be read quickly, nor should it be read only once. Sit in this book for the rest of your life and feast on rich truths concerning Jesus Christ, our King.

> "How great a happiness must it be to be the object of the love of Him who is the Creator of the world, by whom all things consist, who is exalted at God's right hand, and made head over principalities and powers in heavenly places, who has all things put under His feet, who is King of kings and Lord of lords, and is the

---

23. Edwards, Jonathan. Collected and Edited by Don Kistler. *Altogether Lovely*. (Morgan, Penn.: Soli Deo Gloria Publications, 1997), 98.

brightness of the Father's glory! Surely to be beloved by Him is enough to satisfy the soul of a worm of dust."

Gospel Devotional: Truth Seven

1) Review Previous Truths
Truth One: God is the sovereign Creator of all things.

Truth Two: God created people for His glory.

Truth Three: God is holy and righteous.

Truth Four: Man is sinful.

Truth Five: God is just and is right to punish sin.

Truth Six: God is merciful. He is kind to undeserving sinners.

2) Truth Seven
Jesus is God's holy and righteous Son.

3) Supportive Scripture
John 1:1, 14; I Timothy 1:15

Read these passages of Scripture as well as any other Scripture that you know of that supports the truth that Jesus is God's holy and righteous Son.

4) Explanation
How did God make a way for sin to be punished and for sinners to be saved? He did it by sending His only Son, Jesus, into the world. Because Jesus is the Son of God, He is fully God. That means everything true of God the Father, is true of Jesus, God the Son. For example, Jesus is all-powerful, just like God the Father is all-powerful. That is why Jesus could do things like healing

sick people, making crippled people walk, making blind men see, and bringing dead people back to life.

However, when God sent Jesus to live on this earth, God also had Jesus become fully human. That is why Jesus was born as a real baby and grew up like real boys do and became a grown man. Because Jesus became a real person like you and me, He knows what it is like to be sleepy and hungry. He understands what it is like to learn to walk, run, read, and write. He knows how hard it can be to trust and obey God all the time. Even though Jesus became just like us in all these ways, He was able to do something we could never, ever do: Jesus never once sinned! Because He is God's Son, Jesus was born without a sin nature, without the desire to sin. Even when the devil tempted Him to sin, Jesus never sinned. Jesus perfectly obeyed God's holy, righteous, and good commands all the time! Jesus is holy and righteous. This is great news for sinners!

5) **Illustration**

   a) *Make a list*

   With the help of your child, fill up a piece of paper, line by line, with a long list of sins. Take your time with this—fill the whole page. When you are satisfied that the list is full, one by one ask the question, "Did Jesus do this?" Answer: No. As you answer "no," cross out that sin until all the sins are crossed out.

   Optional way to do the above illustration: Use erasable markers and a large mirror or whiteboard to make your list. Erase the sins as you say "no."

6) **What does this mean**
   Jesus came into the world to save you.

Additional Helps: Truth Seven

Additional Reading

Matthew 3:1-17; Matthew 17:1-8; and John 1:1-34

Prayer Prompts

- What does it mean that Jesus is holy? Talk about it, then tell Him in prayer.
- Read Hebrews 7:26-27. Jesus is the perfect high priest who never sinned. He is holy and righteous. Take time to consider what that means; He never had a bad attitude—ever. There was never even a fraction of a second of the "smallest" sin in his heart—ever.
- Read Philippians 2:9-11. We see that God lifts up what name above every other name? Praise that name in prayer.

A Prayer of Blessing for Truth Seven

> "May God do whatever it takes in your heart so that you would honor and worship the name of Jesus
>
> May you be blessed with a right view of the gospel
>
> May your understanding of the cross grow
>
>> And may it strengthen your adoration for Jesus
>
> Jesus is holy
>
>> May you worship Him
>
> Jesus is righteous
>
> He is supremely passionate for what is supremely glorious: His Father's glory

> May you lift Him up from deep in your heart

Jesus is God's holy and righteous Son

> May you lift up His holy name with the highest of admiration, respect and honor"

A Word for Parents

John Owen's book *The Glory of Christ*[25] is an illuminating work that stokes the fires of our affection for Jesus Christ. This quote is taken from the version that contains his abbreviated work but preserves the essence of his intent. This is John Owen made accessible to us, for he should be read.

> "Christ is the meat, the bread, the food provided by God for your soul. And there is no higher spiritual nourishment in Christ than his mediatory love, and this you should always desire. In his love, Christ is glorious. No creatures, angels or men could have the least idea of it before it was revealed by Christ. And after it was seen in this world, it is still absolutely incomprehensible."

Gospel Devotional: Truth Eight

1) Review Previous Truths

Truth One: God is the sovereign Creator of all things.

Truth Two: God created people for His glory.

Truth Three: God is holy and righteous.

Truth Four: Man is sinful.

Truth Five: God is just and is right to punish sin.

---

25. Owen, John. Abridged by R.J.K. Law. *The Glory of Christ*, (Carlisle, Penn.: The Banner of Truth Trust, 1994), 56.

Truth Six: God is merciful. He is kind to undeserving sinners.

Truth Seven: Jesus is God's holy and righteous Son.

2) **Truth Eight**
   God put the punishment of sinners on Jesus, so that His righteousness might be put on them.

3) **Supportive Scripture**
   Isaiah 53:5; Romans 5:8; 2 Corinthians 5:21; and 1 Peter 2:24

   Read these passages of Scripture as well as any other Scripture that you know of that supports the truth that God put the punishment of sinners on Jesus.

4) **Explanation**
   Our biggest problem is that we are sinners who deserve to be punished by God for sin with death and hell. However, because God is merciful, He made a way for sin to be punished and for sinners to be saved. How did He do this? God sent Jesus into the world to save helpless sinners. How could Jesus do this? Jesus is fully God. He did something that you or I or anyone else could never do: Jesus obeyed all God's commands, all the time. Jesus never sinned; He is perfectly holy and righteous. How does this help sinners?

   Since Jesus is holy and righteous and has no sin of His own, He was able to be the perfect substitute for sinners. What is a substitute? A substitute is someone who takes the place of someone else. For example, a substitute teacher takes the place of your teacher when he is absent. A baby-sitter takes the place of mom and dad when they are gone.

Jesus acted as a substitute for sinners by taking the place of sinners. How? Jesus was willing to take the punishment for all the sins of His people. Jesus received from God the punishment that His people deserved. This is what Jesus did by dying on the cross. This is what God sent Jesus into the world to do. That is why Jesus was hung on a cross, so that God, His Father, could punish Jesus instead of having to punish His people. When Jesus died on the cross in place of His sinful people, He experienced all the terrible anger and hatred God has toward their sin.

Not only did Jesus take away the sin and punishment of His people so our sins would be forgiven, Jesus also gave something to His people, something you and I need in order to go to heaven and live forever with God. What did Jesus give His people? His perfect righteousness! Remember, God says that we must be holy and righteous and we must obey Him all the time. Jesus always obeyed God; Jesus is righteous and holy. When Jesus died on the cross He took away the sin and punishment of His people, and then gave to them His perfect righteousness!

Jesus' death on the cross was not the end of the story however. After Jesus died, He was buried. But guess what? Jesus did not stay buried. He was resurrected from the dead. That means He rose from the dead and came alive again! Jesus' resurrection is proof He has won the battle over sin and death and hell. Because of this, God's people are now saved so they can someday go to heaven and live with Him and enjoy Him forever! Jesus is a living Savior. There is no one like Jesus!

5) **Illustration**

   a) *Two Backpacks*
   Collect two backpacks. Put the first backpack on your child and slowly fill it up with lots of heavy stuff until the child begins to feel "weighed down" under the burden of carrying it. Place a sign on it that says "MY SIN." Explain to your child that your sin is something like carrying a very heavy sack. It weighs you down and is a burden to carry.

   Next, give the child a sign that says, "GOD'S PUNISHMENT." What is the right punishment for our sin? Death and hell. Remind the child that this is what we deserve because of our sin.

   Then have dad wear a name-tag that says "JESUS" and explain that dad is going to play the part of Jesus for a minute. Using the second backpack, put a sign on this empty backpack saying "NO SIN = HOLY AND RIGHTEOUS" and have dad put it on. Jesus had no sin of His own. Jesus was perfectly righteous and holy.

   Read and act out Isaiah 53:5, 2 Corinthians 5:21, or 1 Peter 2:24 by having dad remove the heavy backpack from his child. Have dad then place his empty pack on the child. Next, have dad place the heavy pack on himself and take the "GOD'S PUNISHMENT" sign from the child and holding it.

   This can help us to understand what Jesus did for sinners on the cross. He takes the sin of His people and is punished in their place. And He gives (imputes) to sinners His perfect righteousness.

b) Math Test
Create a hard math test for your child. Make sure that it is impossible to get any answers right.

Have you or your spouse take the test with your child, but make sure you get all the answers right and your child gets all the answers wrong. Before they turn in their tests, instruct them to write their names on the test. Then grade the test: Your child gets an "F." Your spouse gets an "A." Give your spouse a prize for doing so well. Do not give a prize to your child.

After handing back their tests and handing out the prize, ask for the tests back. Cross out their names and write in each other's names, switching them. Give the "A" test to your child. Give the "F" test to your spouse. Take the prize back from your spouse and give it to your child.

This can help us to better understand what Jesus did for sinners on the cross. He took our inability to perfectly obey God (our "incorrect answers") and the punishment that we deserve (our "F") and gives to sinners His perfect righteousness (dad or mom's all correct answers) and His reward (dad or mom's "A" score, which earned the prize).

6) Implication
Jesus died on the cross to be punished in your place.

Additional Helps: Truth Eight

Additional Reading

Isaiah 53; Galatians 3:13

Prayer Prompts

- Read through Isaiah 53 and then pray. You might even consider not saying anything after reading, just move right into prayer.
- A danger for us is that we would get used to Jesus being our substitute. Pray for hearts to always be sensitive and to this truth.

A Prayer of Blessing for Truth Eight

> "May your heart feel—as you think about Jesus' death in your place
>
>> He became a curse—for you
>>
>> He was made to be sin—for you
>
> May you see how bad sin is, because of what God had to do to fix this problem
>
>> He gave His best—for you
>>
>> He gave His Son Jesus—for you
>
> So, may your heart always be moved, whenever you hear these words:
>
>> "He was wounded for our transgressions"
>>
>> "He was cursed for our iniquities"
>>
>> "Upon Him was the chastisement that brought us peace"

"And with His stripes we are healed"

A Word for Parents

Dennis Gundersen's book *Your Child's Profession of Faith*[26] is a very helpful assist to parents as they seek to discern grace upon their child's heart. This book is practical, but it is also very insightful in exposing the hidden pits that are often found in the pursuit of conversion with young children.

> *"Urge Christ-centeredness, not profession-centeredness. One of the worst mistakes parents can make is to permit their child to become preoccupied with anguish over his standing in the church and whether he is a baptized member yet or not. Urge him instead to focus all his attention on knowing Jesus Christ, his Lord, to whom alone he will give account!"*

Gospel Devotional: Truth Nine

1) Review Previous Truths

Truth One: God is the sovereign Creator of all things.

Truth Two: God created people for His glory.

Truth Three: God is holy and righteous.

Truth Four: Man is sinful.

Truth Five: God is just and is right to punish sin.

Truth Six: God is merciful. He is kind to undeserving sinners.

Truth Seven: Jesus is God's holy and righteous Son.

---

26. Gundersen, Dennis. *Your Child's Profession of Faith*. (Amityville, NY: Calvary Press, 1994), 50.

Truth Eight: God put the punishment of sinners on Jesus.

2) Truth Nine

God offers the free gift of salvation to those who repent and believe in Jesus.

3) Scripture

Mark 1:15; John 3:16-17; Acts 4:12; Ephesians 2:8-9

Read these passages of Scripture as well as any other Scripture that you know of that supports the truth that God offers the free gift of salvation to those who repent and believe in Jesus.

4) Explanation

Jesus came into the world to save sinners from death and hell so we could go to heaven and live with God forever. Salvation means "to save" someone. Because of what Jesus did, God now wants to give sinners the free gift of salvation. Salvation is like a wonderful gift; in fact, it is the best present you could ever receive! Salvation is a free gift because it is something you do not deserve and could never earn or work for. Jesus did all the work for you!

Does this mean that all people are saved from death and hell because of what Jesus has done? Does it mean that as long as you know the story about what Jesus did on the cross, you will be saved? How can you and I get this free gift from God? God gives salvation to everyone who repents of his sins and believes in Jesus. When God decides to save a sinner, He brings about a change in his heart. What is this change? It is repentance and belief. To repent means you understand you are a helpless sinner who deserves the punishment of death and hell. You feel terrible about your sin and your disobedience to God—you hate your own sin, your sin nature, and sin of all kinds. You want to turn away from your sin and look to Jesus for forgiveness.

Believing in Jesus means you believe true things about Him. You believe He is God's Son. You believe He never sinned. You believe that when He died on the cross, He was punished in your place. You believe He rose from the dead and is living in heaven today. You believe that He alone can save you and bring you to heaven to live with God forever.

But believing in Jesus is not just about knowing and agreeing with true things about Jesus. For example, I can believe someone is a good pilot, but if I am afraid to get on his plane and fly with him, I am showing I do not really believe in his ability as a pilot. If I believe he is a good pilot, I should trust in his ability to fly the airplane and not be afraid.

That is a little like what it means to "believe in Jesus." It means you are trusting Him to save your life. You are depending on Him. You are placing all of your confidence in Him. You believe He died on the cross for you, not just for other people. You believe He will bring you to heaven to live forever with God. If you are really trusting in Jesus, you will repent of your sins and trust Jesus to save you. Repentance and belief always go together.

5) **Illustration**

Note: this illustration is regarding trust/trusting in someone.

Collect a whistle, a raw egg, a small plate, a small prize (such as a piece of candy), and a better prize (like a bag of candy).

Set the plate on a table and then place the egg on the plate. Give your child the smaller prize to hold. Hold the whistle in your hand and then make the following promise to your child: "I will give you this whistle to use. If you blow the whistle exactly three times, this egg <u>will break</u> and then I will give you this bigger and better prize. That is my promise. However, if the egg doesn't break, not only will you not get the bigger and better prize, you will also have to give back the smaller prize."

Ask, does this seem like a silly idea? Do eggs break because someone blows a whistle three times? Then ask, "Do you believe my promise? If you are confident that I will keep my promise, what will you do?" When your child does exactly as instructed and blows the whistle three times, pick up the egg and release it from about two feet above the plate so that it drops and breaks.

Ask your child, "Ultimately, was it the whistle that broke the egg? No. Was it the fact that you blew the whistle three times that broke the egg? No. Was it you who broke the egg? No. It was I (mom or dad) who broke the egg in <u>response</u> to your <u>trust in me</u> to keep my promise. And who gave you the whistle so that you were able to respond to my promise? I did."

This can help us to better understand true, saving faith. Faith is like the whistle that we blow three times. It is a response of confidence in the One who made the promise. God has made a promise: Whoever trusts in Jesus will be saved. Faith is the response of confidence in the One who made this promise. True saving faith is not about having any confidence in ourselves to bring about our salvation (as in trusting in the whistle itself or our ability to blow it). Ultimately, it is not OUR faith that saves us, as if faith is some kind work that we do. Rather it is the object of that faith—JESUS—that saves us. God saves sinners in response to their trusting in Jesus. And just as the whistle was given to the child by his parent, true saving faith is a gift from God. Salvation is by grace alone, through faith alone, in Christ Jesus alone!

6) Implication

God tells you to believe in Jesus and repent of your sins and you will be saved.

Additional Helps: Truth Nine

Additional Reading

Isaiah 55:1-3; Acts 26:12-28; and 2 Timothy 2:22-26

Prayer Prompts

- Read John 3:1-21 and use it as a prayer guide.

- Talk about what repentance and belief mean. For example, believing a chair will hold you up, and believing it will hold you up to the point of actually sitting down on it are two different things.

- Read John 15:1-5 and ask God to do whatever it takes in your heart, so you would listen to Jesus, love Him, come to Him, abide in Him, repent of sin, and believe in Him. (Note: if you have already repented and believed, then fruit of that will be continued repentance and belief.)

A Prayer of Blessing for Truth Nine:

"May you join those who have repented of sin and have believed in Jesus

> *May you trust in Him*
>
> *May you abide in Him*
>
> *May you listen to Him*
>
> *May you love Him*
>
> *May you come to Him*
>
> *May you be glad to belong to Jesus*

For He is the One who has become your substitute—a perfect substitute

Yes indeed, may you repent and believe and keep on repenting and believing"

A Word for Parents

John Piper's book *What Jesus Demands from the World*[27] is made up of many short chapters. The first eight are particularly pointed to both justification and continued sanctification. For example, he writes to the unsaved, "listen to Jesus," and to the saved, "keep listening to Jesus." Thus it is that even as believing parents urge their children to faith, they are to be assessing their own hearts. Please invest time in reading this book in its entirety.

> *"I urge you on behalf of Jesus, listen to his word. Be like Mary and sit at his feet (Luke 10:39, 42). Don't*

---

27. Piper, John. *What Jesus Demands from the World.* (Wheaton, Ill.: Crossway Books, 2006), 61.

turn away from the command of his Father given on the Mount of Transfiguration: "This is my beloved Son, with whom I am well pleased; listen to him" (Matt. 17:5) [. . . .] Don't hate yourself by rejecting the one who said, "these things I have spoken to you [. . .] that your joy may be full" (John 15:11; cf. 17:13). Listen to Jesus."

Gospel Devotional: Truth Ten

1) Review Previous Truths

Truth One: God is the sovereign Creator of all things.

Truth Two: God created people for His glory.

Truth Three: God is holy and righteous.

Truth Four: Man is sinful.

Truth Five: God is just and is right to punish sin.

Truth Six: God is merciful. He is kind to undeserving sinners.

Truth Seven: Jesus is God's holy and righteous Son.

Truth Eight: God put the punishment of sinners on Jesus.

Truth Nine: God offers the free gift of salvation to those who repent and believe in Jesus.

2) Truth Ten

Those who trust in Jesus will live to please Him and will receive the promise of eternal life—enjoying God forever in heaven.

3) Scripture

Luke 9:23; John 11:25; 1 John 2:15; Psalm 16:11

Read these passages of Scripture as well as any other Scripture that you know of that supports the truth that those who trust in Jesus will live to please Him and will receive the promise of eternal life—enjoying God forever in heaven.

4) Explanation

If you want to play the piano or be on a baseball team, would you expect it would take a certain amount of time and practice? Would it be a good thing to think about this before you started piano lessons or joined the baseball team? Why? Because there is a "cost" involved to the choices we make. If you want to play the piano well, it will demand your time because you will have to practice. You will need to give up other things in order to practice and to go to lessons. What might you have to give up in order to play the piano well? What will you need to change in order to be a good baseball player?

Salvation is a free gift offered to you by God and it is given to everyone who truly repents and is trusting in Jesus. But this free gift will cost you your whole life! What does that mean? It means you must do things Jesus' way instead of your own way. It means every day you must trust and follow Jesus for the rest of your life—when you're 10, 20, 50, and even 90 years old. In order to do this, there are things you will have to give up and things you will need to change.

For example, you will need to spend time praying instead of just playing. You will need to spend time reading your Bible instead of just watching television.

You will need to spend time thinking about God instead of just thinking about friends. That is hard work! Have you thought about the "cost" of trusting in Jesus? Are you ready to truly repent and trust Jesus and then do things His way for the rest of your life? Even when you get old?

God has a promise for everyone who is trusting in Jesus: He will give you a special Helper, the Holy Spirit. The Holy Spirit is God and He lives inside every person who trusts in Jesus. The Holy Spirit is all-powerful and He is there to help you with the hard work of doing things Jesus' way. The Holy Spirit will begin to change you, so you love, trust, obey, and enjoy God more and more.

There is a cost to following Jesus, but God has promised a huge reward for everyone who trusts in Jesus—a reward that is so great and exciting that it is better than anything we can even imagine. What is it? Eternal life! Eternal life is living forever with God in heaven. Heaven is a real place where everyone who is trusting in Jesus will someday go to live. God's people will not sin anymore. Our bodies will be perfect. No more being sick, or dying, or feeling hurt or lonely. There will be no bad things in heaven. Everything will be clean and perfect and beautiful, but those things aren't even the best part of heaven. The best part of heaven is that God will live there with His people. We will finally get to really see Jesus! There is nothing and no one who is more amazing, great, wonderful, beautiful, and exciting than Jesus. Being with Jesus will make us happy forever.

5) Illustration

Use daily illustrations from life to talk about the joy of heaven: When your children turn to something that they think is great, fun, amazing, etc., remind them that being with Jesus forever will be a million times better. Use the anticipation of seeing a friend or grandparent after a long absence to talk about the joy that God's children will have in seeing Jesus some day. It will be a zillion times better.

6) Implication

If you are trusting in Jesus for your salvation, you must follow Him. Jesus has promised that when you die He will bring you to heaven to live with God and enjoy Him forever.

Additional Helps: Truth Ten

Additional Reading

Matthew 25:1-30; John 12:20-26; 1 John 2:4-6, 5:1-5

Prayer Prompts

- Read John 12:20-26. Why is the exaltation of Jesus and His death brought together here? Following Jesus means going where He went. Where did He go? What does it mean for His followers? Find the answers in these verses.
- Can you imagine what it must be like, to hear your Master, Jesus, say "enter into the joy of your master" (Matthew 25:21-23)? Pray for this, that it would happen to each and everyone in your home.

A Prayer of Blessing for Truth Ten

> "May you be numbered with those who belong to Jesus and may you affirm it

> By following Him in life
>
> By following Him in death
>
>> May you live and die for His sake, and may you be glad to do so
>
> May you be blessed to hear these words from your Savior and King
>
>> Enter into the joy of your Master
>
> May it be your joy to trust and obey Jesus now in this life
>
>> May it not be a burden but the joy of your heart
>
>> May you know peace in following Him
>
>> May you love others as you follow Him
>
> May the first fruits of joy now excite your heart as you long for pure everlasting joy with Jesus in heaven"

A Word for Parents

Charles Spurgeon's book *The Power of the Cross of Christ*[28] is not a book to read once; rather it is a book to live with. It is full of Gospel truth and Gospel calling. It is also very helpful to read as you prepare to eat and drink the Lord's Supper: this is a call to remember and to do so with passion in your heart for your King.

> *"I beseech you repent of your sin, bewail your condition, and fly to Christ for shelter. And if it is your child, give heaven no rest, plead continually at the throne of grace till you have brought down a blessing from God upon your offspring. Never cease to pray until your sons and your daughters are safe landed on the Rock of Ages and so secured there they will need*

---

28. Spurgeon, Charles. *The Power of the Cross of Christ*. (Lynnwood, Wash.: Emerald Books, 1995), 57.

no other rock to hide them in the day when Christ shall come."

Ten Gospel Truths

- *Truth One:* God is the sovereign Creator of all things
- *Truth Two:* God created people for His glory.
- *Truth Three:* God is holy and righteous.
- *Truth Four:* Man is sinful.
- *Truth Five:* God is just and is right to punish sin.
- *Truth Six:* God is merciful. He is kind to undeserving sinners.
- *Truth Seven:* Jesus is God's holy and righteous Son.
- *Truth Eight:* God put the punishment of sinners on Jesus.
- *Truth Nine:* God offers the free gift of salvation to those who repent and believe in Jesus.
- *Truth Ten:* Those who trust in Jesus will live to please Him and will receive the promise of eternal life—enjoying God forever in heaven.

Recommended Titles for Further Reading

From "Preparing Children for the Gospel"

- *Faith of a Child* by Art Murphy (Moody Press)
- *Repentance and Faith* by Charles Walker (Solid Ground Christian Books)
- *The Child's Book of Repentance* by Thomas H. Gallaudet (Solid Ground Christian Books)
- *The Pastor's Daughter* by Louisa Payson Hopkins (Solid Ground Christian Books)
- *Your Child's Profession of Faith* by Dennis Gundersen (Calvary Press)
- *Tell the Truth* by Will Metzger (InterVarsity Press)
- *Feed My Lambs* by John Todd (Solid Ground Christian Books), especially chapters on faith and repentance
- *Lectures to My Students* by Charles Spurgeon, especially chapter on conversion
- *Systematic Theology* by Wayne Grudem (Zondervan), especially Section 5

From "Presenting the Gospel to Children"

- *Tell the Truth* by Will Metzger (InterVarsity Press)
- *God Is the Gospel* by John Piper (Crossway Books)
- *The Gospel According to Jesus* by John MacArthur (Zondervan)

About Truth78

Truth78 is a vision-oriented ministry for the next generations. Our vision is that the next generations know, honor, and treasure God, setting their hope in Christ alone, so that they will live as faithful disciples for the glory of God.

Our mission is to nurture the faith of the next generations by equipping the church and home with resources and training that instruct the mind, engage the heart, and influence the will through proclaiming the whole counsel of God.

Values that undergird the development of our resources and training are that they be God-centered, Bible-saturated, Gospel-focused, Christ-exalting, Spirit-dependent, doctrinally grounded, and discipleship-oriented.

Resources for Church and Home

Truth78 currently offers the following categories of resources and training materials for equipping the church and home:

Vision-Casting and Training

We offer a wide variety of booklets, video and audio seminars, articles, and other practical training resources that highlight and further expound our vision, mission, and values, as well as our educational philosophy and methodology. Many of these resources are freely distributed through our website. These resources and training serve to assist ministry leaders, volunteers, and parents in implementing Truth78's vision and mission in their churches and homes.

Curriculum

We publish materials designed for formal Bible instruction. The scope and sequence of these materials reflects our commitment to teach children and youth the whole counsel of God over the course of their education. Materials include curricula for Sunday school, Midweek Bible programs, Backyard Bible Clubs or Vacation Bible School, and Intergenerational studies. Most of these materials can be adapted for use in Christian schools and education in the home.

Parenting and Family Discipleship

We have produced a variety of materials and training resources designed to help parents in their role in discipling their children. These include booklets, video presentations, family devotionals, children's books, articles, and other recommended resources. Furthermore, our curricula include Growing in Faith Together (GIFT) Pages to help parents apply what is taught in the classroom to their child's daily experience in order to nurture faith.

Bible Memory

Our Fighter Verses Bible memory program is designed to encourage churches, families, and individuals in the lifelong practice and love of Bible memory. The Fighter Verses program utilizes an easy-to-use Bible memory system with carefully chosen verses to help fight the fight of faith. It is available in print, on FighterVerses.com, and as an app for smart phones and other mobile devices. The Fighter Verses App includes review reminders, quizzes, songs, a devotional, and other memory helps. For pre-readers, Foundation Verses uses simple images to help young children memorize 76 key verses. We also offer a study, devotional guide, and coloring book that correspond to Set 1 of the Fighter Verses. Visit FighterVerses.com for the weekly devotional blog and for free memory aids.

For more information on any of these resources contact:

Truth78.org
info@Truth78.org
1-877-400-1414
@Truth78org